CLAUDE MONET

CAPTURING LIGHT AND NATURE

by Mick Manning and Brita Granström

FRANKLIN WATTS

LONDON • SYDNEY

Contents

Turn the page and discover how painting became my life ...

Mother Nature was my first art teacher!

Growing Up by the Sea

"... it was such a joy to run about on the cliffs!"

Did you know that all colour is made of light? Well, of course I didn't
know that as a child either, and yet even so I soon became aware that the
very air was made of delicious colours: violet, blue, indigo, pink, yellow,
green ... In 1845, when I was five years old, my Parisian parents took
me to live beside the sea at Le Havre in Normandy, and, as I grew older,
I often went exploring along the beaches and cliffs with my sketchbook.
I was good at pencil drawing and I would return home mercilessly
scratched by brambles and stung by nettles. You could say that Mother
Nature was my first art teacher ...

Eugène Boudin

"From my most tender infancy I already had a passion for drawing."

My second teacher was a landscape painter named Eugène Boudin. As a teenager I often drew caricatures of local people and, at seventeen, I had my first exhibition in a local picture framer's shop that Boudin used. When he saw my cartoons he said, "These little things are yours are they, young man?" In his gentle way he was telling me that I could do much better. In fact, he invited me to go painting outdoors with him. At first, in my ignorance, I was unimpressed by Boudin's paintings. To my uneducated eye they looked half-finished and scribbly. Nevertheless, it was Boudin who persuaded me to buy my first paintbox.

Jules Didier with Wings, c.1860
Monet drew this caricature of the landscape painter, Jules Didier, with a butterfly's body.

Monet's caricatures were influenced by humorists such as Étienne Carjat, Honoré Daumier and others he saw published in newspapers and the popular satirical comic *Le Charivari*. His caricatures began as doodles in his schoolbooks but became so popular that Monet began to sell them for 20 francs each.

Meeting Eugène Boudin was a turning point in Monet's life. Boudin took Monet under his wing and encouraged him to focus his natural talent on painting landscapes.

En Plein Air

"I haven't forgotten that you were the first to teach me to see and understand."

Outdoors with Boudin, watching him in action and painting *en plein air*, I suddenly understood his genius. As I set to work beside him I found oil painting was difficult. To a beginner like me it felt like painting with tubes of greasy toothpaste! But Boudin patiently began to show me how to mix colours and how, by painting 'wet on wet' like him, I could capture what I saw. This generous man became not only my mentor but a friend who would teach me about the science of light and colour – and this knowledge made sure that capturing nature's colour and light would become my life's work …

Tubes of Paint

Oil paint is made of pigment (coloured powders) mixed with a slow-drying oil such as linseed oil. It is traditionally mixed or 'thinned' with turpentine, a spirit made from the resin of pine trees. Before John Rand invented squeezable, ready-mixed tubes of paint in 1841, artists had to grind up the pigments and mix their own paints.

Traditional techniques taught that every layer of paint should dry before adding another. It could take hours or even days. Boudin was a rebel who encouraged Monet to paint en plein air, which means 'in the open air'. He taught Monet to paint 'wet on wet' – adding and mixing layers of wet paint, one on top of another, to capture ever-changing weather and light.

Colour theory

The primary colours of paint are red, yellow and blue. When they mix they make new 'secondary' colours. For example red and yellow paint mix to make orange, and if you mix all the colours together you get black. Monet learned that rays of light mix very differently to create the colours our eyes see in nature. The primary colours of light are red, green and blue. When red and green light mix they create yellow and if you mix all the colours together you get white light!

As early as the mid-1600s, the scientist Sir Isaac Newton proved with his experiments that colours are made by different wavelengths of light.

Try mixing coloured paints together yourself and see what colours you make.

Paint or printing ink colour wheel

Light colour wheel

Paris and Algeria

"As for my stay in Algeria, I was entranced by it."

By 1859, having learned much from Boudin, I had enrolled at the Académie Suisse in Paris, a cheaply priced art academy. Here, the drawing classes bustled with artists of every description and not only was I free to pester them with questions, I also made sure that I got answers. This is where I first met my friend Camille Pissarro, a man who would become a leading Impressionist painter.

But then, in 1861, my name was selected for military service and I was shipped off to Algeria, an African country that was under French control. I can't begin to tell you how much I hated being ordered around in that boring military camp. Luckily for me I became so ill that they sent me home.

Monet was stationed in Algeria but didn't like it at all ...

A story tells that he grew so frustrated being stuck in the barracks that one day he galloped out of the gates on a captured mule. But he didn't get far before falling off ...

When Monet was found by a rescue party his uniform was torn to shreds. He was diagnosed with typhoid fever and so was spared a court martial for deserting his post.

***Hauling a Boat Ashore, Honfleur*, 1864**
When home in Normandy, before returning to Paris, Monet had met and befriended the good-natured Dutch painter Johan Jongkind. This painting shows Honfleur, a seaside town in Normandy, where they would paint together, en plein air. In Monet's own words, Jongkind 'completed the teachings I had already received from Boudin'.

The Dandy

"Not a penny left ... no more credit at the butcher's or the baker's ..."

I returned to Paris; this time studying at Monsieur Gleyre's studio. My new artist friends included: Édouard Manet, Paul Cézanne, Alfred Sisley, Pierre-Auguste Renoir and the stubborn man who was to become my dearest friend, Frédéric Bazille. Manet introduced us to the bustling Café Guerbois in the Batignolles district near his studio. We would all sit together for hours discussing art and politics. Even though I had very little money in those days, I dressed as fashionably as I could and this led to my new friends giving me the nickname – 'the dandy'.

Café Guerbois, in the Batignolles district, was one of many bustling Parisian cafes. It became a meeting place for a group of bohemian artists who would become known as 'The Batignolles'. Led by Manet, it also included Claude Monet, Alfred Sisley, Frédéric Bazille, Pierre-Auguste Renoir, Camille Pissarro, Paul Cézanne, Edgar Degas and Berthe Morisot. Morisot was one of very few female painters. It seems ridiculous now, but women were not allowed to attend art classes in those days.

Picnic in the Garden

"I'm not performing miracles, I'm using up and wasting a lot of paint ..."

Living in Paris, trying to make money as a painter, I soon discovered
how hard it was. When I began a painting I called *Picnic in the Garden*,
a canvas that stood over 2 metres tall, I was dismayed to see it use up
so much of my expensive paint tubes. In the end I never finished it but
gave it to my landlord instead of paying the rent I owed him. When
I was able to buy it back many years later the canvas was so badly
damaged by damp that I could only salvage pieces of it ... but such is
life, or, as we say in France, *'C'est la vie'*!

Picnic in the Garden **(central section), 1866**
This fragment of Monet's unfinished painting reminds us that
artists paint to experiment and to learn by their mistakes. Monet
painted this after seeing Édouard Manet's 1863 painting *The Bath*.
Claude Monet was exploring folded fabric and dappled forest light.
He was also perhaps exploring how Manet had painted his own
masterpiece and there is no doubt he learned a lot by doing so. In
fact, after seeing Monet's painting Manet changed the name of his
own painting *The Bath* to *Picnic in the Garden*. The original painting
was huge, as you can see in our artist's reconstruction on the left.
This is based on a sketch in the care of The Pushkin Museum.

Camille

"The weather is fine but there is a devil of a wind ..."

We Batignolles would encourage one another to push against the boundaries that the 'bourgeois' art critics and galleries put in our way. In 1870, I married Camille Doncieux. She had been my artists' model for many years and one day, while painting her sitting with Boudin's wife Marie-Anne on a Normandy beach, the wind became so gusty that sand not only blew into our eyes, but also became trapped in the wet paint on the canvas. I let it be and to this day, those grains of sand remain in my painting, preserved forever with my darling Camille. Now that is what I call en plein air painting!

***The Beach at Trouville,* 1870**

This painting of Camille Doncieux, sitting with her friend Madame Boudin, is bespattered with sand that has blown onto the canvas and become glued by the oil paint. Far from spoiling the painting, it adds a feeling of authenticity and atmosphere to Monet's painting and bears witness to the unpredictability of painting en plein air!

London

After our marriage, Camille and I fled to London to avoid the Franco-
Prussian war that would kill my dear friend Bazille. I fell in love with that
dirty city and how the Sun flickered colours through the layers of fog and
smoke that hovered above the filthy River Thames. In the London art
galleries, I discovered the paintings of Monsieur J. M. W. Turner such as
Rain, Steam and Speed. The rain! The steam! The speed! It was all there for
the eye to see! Turner's understanding of how light shone through smoke
and steam was inspiring.

The Thames Below Westminster, 1871
The River Thames was so heavily polluted with sewage that in 1858 the smell had been so unbearable that even the Houses of Parliament had to close in a summer that was called The Great Stink. However the light reflecting through the fog and rain, and how it lit the buildings, bridges and water with diffused colours, fascinated Monet. He had to paint quickly and yet this haste, far from making the paintings sketchy or lacking detail as you might expect, actually helps add a sense of movement.

The Impressionists

"People must first of all learn to look at Nature and only then may they see and understand what we are trying to do ..."

Me and my painter friends grew so frustrated with our paintings being mostly rejected by The Salon, the most important national art exhibition, that in 1874, we held our own exhibition! When the newspaper critics came along they mocked us, just as we expected. One even wrote that we were 'lunatics' and singled out my own painting *Impression, Sunrise,* sarcastically dismissing it as 'nothing more than an impression'. Up to that day we had called ourselves the Batignolles … but from then on we turned the haters into motivators by giving ourselves a new name - *The Impressionists!*

The exhibition was held in a Paris photographer's studio. Alongside Claude Monet were Alfred Sisley, Eugène Boudin, Pierre-Auguste Renoir, Camille Pissarro, Paul Cézanne, Edgar Degas and Berthe Morisot. Édouard Manet chose not to exhibit.

Impression, Sunrise, 1872

Monet captured the impression of a sunrise in Le Havre by painting quickly and using both thick daubs and scribbly brushstrokes of oil paint. To the art critics, who wrote for the newspapers, and who expected to see highly finished, realistic landscapes, Monet's painting looked unfinished and careless. No one thought to look closely at how Monet had captured the light.

Camille and Jean

"The further I get the more I regret how little I know."

In 1875 I made a family portrait. Not like the dull, old fashioned ones that were posed indoors and so boring you could almost hear the clock ticking! No, my portrait showed my dear wife and son out for a stroll. As they posed for me on the top of a small hillock I had to work quickly to keep things fresh, using thick brushstrokes of oil paint to capture Camille's veil fluttering in the breeze and the light streaming across their clothes. If you look closely, you will see my son, hands in his pockets, impatient to go off and explore, just like I was at his age.

***Woman with a Parasol – Madame Monet and Her Son*, 1875**
This portrait might remind you of a modern smartphone snapshot from social media. It beautifully records a moment of family life. Monet has used quick brushstrokes to quickly capture Madame Monet. Her parasol and veil protect her from the Sun. Monet was so short of money at this time that he eventually gave this painting to his doctor to pay his medical bills.

Floating Studio

"I have just been thrown out of the inn where I was staying, naked as a worm."

Money was always a worry as my painting sales were few and far between thanks to merciless and ignorant newspaper critics putting off gallery buyers. One day, on holiday with my family, I was humiliated to be thrown out of our hotel because I couldn't pay the bill! But despite this, Camille and I managed to acquire a boat which I could use to paint on the river. It had a little cabin, and sometimes friends would join us for tea. In fact Édouard Manet once painted a portrait of us one fine day. Camille and I were never happier than when we were lazily drifting downstream aboard my beloved floating studio.

The Studio Boat, 1876

In this romantic painting Monet shows us his studio boat. Evening is falling and the boat is moving peacefully with the current. He portrays himself crouched in the cabin, at work on the river. He appears practical and down to earth – as if he could just as easily be a hardworking bargeman transporting coal.

Giverny

"... peace of mind is a prerequisite for good work."

Despite my delight at the birth of our second son, Michel, in 1878,
I still had financial worries and owed money seemingly to everyone.
Then the unthinkable happened ... my beloved Camille died. Bereft and
alone, I turned to my friend Alice Hoschedé for comfort. She and her
six children had been living with Camille and I for several years. Alice
and I became very close and, within a few years, we had all settled in a
country house at Giverny with a cheap rent. Oh, how we all loved that
house! It was a new start for me – and for Alice too.

***The Lunch*, 1876-77**

A tranquil garden scene shows Jean playing happily in the shade of the uncleared lunchtime table. Alice Hoschedé and her six children (Blanche, Germaine, Suzanne, Marthe, Jean-Pierre and Jacques), had been living with Claude and Camille at their house in Vétheuil since 1877 after her husband Ernest (once a rich patron of Monet's) had fallen on hard times. Then, after Camille's death, Alice took care of Monet's children as well as her own. In 1892 Claude and Alice were eventually able to marry.

The Yellow Dining Room

Our Home

Giverny became my work of art. Gradually, over the years, as my painting sales began to grow, I would enlarge and decorate it, brightening the interiors with vivid colours! Alice's four daughters had their bedrooms above the kitchen and the four boys slept in the attic rooms. Those young people brought the old house to life with their chatter, as they bustled about from room to room and ran out into the extensive gardens.

The Staircase

The winding stairs with yellow walls led up to the bedrooms.

Suzanne

Blanche

The Tiled Kitchen

The kitchen was tiled in blue with an earth-brown sink.

Monet's Bedroom

My own bedroom had a yellow bed and wardrobe and I had sheets embroidered with my initials!

The Blue Lounge

The living room became a blue, peaceful place. Somewhere to sit with a book or have a nap.

The Big Wave

"I didn't see a huge wave coming; it threw me against the cliff and I was tossed about in its wake ..."

For Alice and myself, moving to Giverny became our love story. However, it was almost a very short story ... One day, while on a painting trip alone beneath a huge sea cliff in Normandy, a huge wave took me unawares and dashed me into the sea. I fought back and when, at last, I managed to drag myself onto the beach I was battered and soaked to the skin. I found my painting lost and my easel broken and yet somehow I had kept a death-grip on my paint palette. In fact, when I finally looked in a mirror I found my beard was smeared with blue and yellow paint!

Stormy Sea in Étretat, 1883
How dangerous those waves look! Painted only a few years earlier, this painting, *Stormy Sea in Étretat*, gives an idea of the cliffs Monet was painting and the stormy sea that almost washed him away. Monet's use of colour, combined with bold brushstrokes, create the feeling of the sea's power and energy, influencing other artists such as Vincent van Gogh.

Grainstacks

"Now I really feel the landscape. I can be bold and include every tone of pink and blue: it's enchanting, it's delicious."

As I said at the beginning of this story, to my artist's eye the very air has always been made of delicious colours and one day I began to think to myself: why just paint a subject once when I could paint the shifting air that surrounded that subject as it changed over time? I visited a field of humble grainstacks near my home and, quite foolishly, only took two canvases with me. But oh! The light was changing so fast that I soon realised I needed many more canvases. Blanche, not only my faithful assistant but also a talented pupil, had to go and fetch a wobbly wheelbarrow piled high with canvases and wheel it to me over the muddy field!

***Grainstacks at Giverny, Sunset*, 1888-89**

Grainstacks were a practical way French farmers
used to preserve harvested grain until needed.
Claude Monet's series of around 25 grainstack
paintings was revolutionary in the atmospheric way
they captured the changing light and how weather
transformed an everyday sight in the countryside.
Monet carefully painted the changes; from glowing
colours of warm summer mornings to the flat cold
hues of winter afternoons. He had as many as
12 paintings on the go each day, moving between
them as the time and light changed. When he
exhibited them in Paris, they were a huge success,
providing a much-needed income for him.

Blanche was Monet's only pupil and
became a talented Impressionist
in her own right. In 1897 she became
his daughter-in-law when she married
her childhood friend, Jean Monet. Her
sister Suzanne often modelled for
Monet's paintings.

My Enchanting Garden

"Don't forget the lily bulbs. Should the Japanese peonies arrive, plant them immediately if weather permits."

After the success of my exhibition of grainstacks in Paris, the art buyers and even the art critics seemed to finally appreciate my paintings. As my sales began to grow I could, at last, afford to buy the house I rented in Giverny and I began to plan flower beds, design walkways and hire gardeners. To me my garden was another sort of artwork, a painting I made with flowers and water, and it was to become my muse, my inspiration.

***Pathway in the Garden of Giverny*, 1902**
Monet hired professional gardeners to work for him and the result was not only a breathtaking garden for him to paint in, but also a supply of fresh flowers to decorate his house. This painting shows the flowerbeds either side of the pathway leading up to his house.

Rouen Cathedral

"Dear God this cursed cathedral is hard to do!"

In February 1892, staying in Rouen, I was taken aback when I opened the shutters of my apartment window to find Rouen's mighty cathedral staring back at me! I began to wonder ... if changing light could transform grainstacks so beautifully, how might it define a solid stone structure? I obtained permission to paint this giant from a fashion boutique because its windows had the best views. There, ignoring the shop's customers, I examined with brush and paint how light can affect the way we see that ancient cathedral's solid shape. Painting and repainting a series of canvases over many visits, just as I had done with my grainstacks, I exhausted myself.

Monet got permission to paint from the window of an old department store across the street.

He chose the window with the best view ...

which happened to be in the ladies' underwear department.

After a while, the store put up some modesty screens at the request of the customers.

Rouen Cathedral, West Facade, 1892

This is just one of over 30 paintings of the cathedral in different weather and at different times of day. Monet uses the 'impasto' technique to great effect – applying thick layers of wet paint to encrust the canvas and give the cathedral's architecture a strong sculptural form. He exhibited them in Paris in 1895. They were incredibly popular and hailed as masterpieces.

The Japanese Bridge

"I will grow plants such as water lilies… which for the most part grow wild along our river and there is thus no question of poisoning the water."

As the years went by, I enlarged my water garden, planting not only wild white water lilies but exotic Egyptian and South American ones as well. At first I had to overcome opposition from a group of locals who thought I might poison their water supply! But I won through, and with my ponds, I began to push myself to new levels, painting the light, the reflections, the lily pads and the sparkling water below the Japanese-style footbridges that I had paid local craftspeople to make for me. My house at Giverny became my outdoor studio and my paintings began to sing like birds! It was enchanting and it was delicious!

Water Lilies and the Japanese Bridge, 1897-98
Monet admired an oriental style and had a huge collection of work
by Japanese printmakers such as Hokusai hanging in his house.
This painting of one of his Japanese bridges is fresh and joyous, full
of light and movement. Green dominates, with shadows in blue.

Return to London

*"In the early hours of this morning there was an extraordinary completely
yellow fog; I did an impression of it."*

I found myself drawn back to London; back to its sulphurous smog and the
eerie red sunsets. But this time I could afford the luxury of the Savoy hotel
and I made sure my room had a view and a balcony to paint from. When the
smog grew too oppressive or the rain chilled me to the bone I would retreat
indoors to continue my paintings through the safely closed windows. I visited
London three times, staying for weeks and making many studies to be finished
later, at home in my studio. When I exhibited the paintings in Paris in 1904
they revealed London like it had never been painted before.

Waterloo Bridge, 1904

Painted from the Savoy hotel one smoggy day, this painting is one of a series
of London paintings made by Monet who would often rise early, before
chimneys began to smoke, and then continue to paint into the gathering
gloom as the smog began to choke the air. In those days the world was
powered by the burning of coal and when the coal smoke mixed with natural
fog rising from the dirty river it created a thick blanket of toxic fumes and
coal smoke called smog. Londoners nicknamed smoggy days 'pea-soupers'.

Loss

"My poor eyesight makes me see everything in a complete fog."

By 1910 the bad times had returned. My eyesight had begun to deteriorate and the gorgeous colours I had loved all my life no longer had the same intensity. I began to wear specially made spectacles but even so, colours began to look muddy and my paintings grew darker. Then my dear wife Alice grew very ill and died, to be followed, only a few years later, by my beloved son Jean. As my mind struggled with the loss and my eyes struggled to see light and shape I came to rely on my poor widowed daughter-in-law Blanche to take care of me. Blanche encouraged me to have an eye operation . . .

The Japanese Footbridge, 1920-22

In 1923, with only ten per cent vision in one of his eyes, Monet agreed to an eye operation. After surgery he could read once more. However his colour vision remained odd, sometimes making his world too blue or too yellow. In this painting we get an idea of how Monet's deteriorating eyesight may have changed the way he saw shape and colour. Look at the dark colours and indistinct shape of the bridge compared to the earlier bridge on page 39.

Water Lilies

"These landscapes of water and reflections have become an obsession."

Water lilies need water to survive, just like I need art! After my eye operation my sight improved and I continued pushing my series of water lily paintings as far as it would go, outpacing my Impressionist colleagues and leading the way into an abstract world of colour. My blobs of paint and sweeping brushstrokes made no sense when viewed close-up, other than being beautiful layers of paint of course. But when viewed from a distance, oh how I loved the fact that it suddenly made sense and my water garden was revealed in all its green, weedy glory for human eyes to enjoy!

***The Water Lilies: Morning with Willows* (close-up detail), 1915-26**
Look closely at this detail from one of Monet's most famous paintings and notice the sweeping brushstrokes and patches of colour . . . but would you know what it was a picture of if you didn't know the title? It looks like a collection of abstract shapes and colours. Now turn the page to see the whole painting and notice how, from a distance, your eye makes sense of it all.

What is abstract?
Abstract art means art that doesn't attempt to portray the world in a realistic way, but uses shapes, colours and textures instead. Works by Cézanne, Braque and some paintings by Picasso are other early examples of Abstract art. Monet's huge water lily paintings use large areas of colour and shape that appear abstract when viewed close-up but, from a distance, work together to achieve a realistic result.

Light and Nature

"I'm enjoying the most perfect tranquility, free from all worries, and in consequence would like to stay this way forever, in a peaceful corner of the countryside."

As the years passed, I became totally absorbed in the light and nature of my lily ponds and continued to paint them even as the First World War raged. When the war ended in 1918 I gave a series of eight of the largest paintings to the French people as symbols of peace and I planned a special room at the Musée de l'Orangerie to house them. The total length of the canvases when hung together side by side is 91 metres and I requested the walls be made curved so that the viewer would be enveloped in my water-world. Now, at 86 years of age, I have to say that I consider these large paintings to be the culmination of my artistic life.

The Water Lilies: Morning with Willows (full image), 1915-26

Over many years Monet painted over 250 stunningly beautiful paintings in his water lily series. Some are so huge it makes the viewer feel they are immersed in the pond. Look back at the detail on the previous page and then look at this full painting in the gallery.

Claude Monet died in 1926 aged 86 and the Monet gallery at the Musée de l'Orangerie was opened the following year.

Franklin Watts
First published 2026
Hodder & Stoughton Limited
Copyright text and illustrations © Mick Manning
and Brita Granström
All rights reserved

Credits:
Editor: Paul Rockett
Design: Peter Scoulding
Picture researcher: Diana Morris

Picture credits:

3: Nympheas, 1918-1926, detail, Musée de L'Orangerie, Paris/ Peter Barrit/Alamy; 7tr: Caricature of Jules Didier c.1858, Art Institute of Chicago; 9c: Light colour wheel/ Lukas Kurka/Shutterstock; 9b: Additive colour mixing/ Lukas Kurka/Dreamstime; 11b: Hauling a Boat Ashore, Honfleur, 4.4.1864/ Wikimedia Commons/Sothebys; 15: The Picnic in the Garden, c.1866, detail, Musée d'Orsay, Paris/ Wikimedia Commons; 17t: The Beach at Trouville, 1870,The National Gallery, London/ incamerastock/Alamy; 19t: The Thames Below Westminster, 1871,The National Gallery, London/ Artefact/Alamy; 21t: Impression, Sunrise, 1872, Musée Marmottan, Paris/ Wikimedia Commons /art database; 23t: Woman with a Parasol-Madame Monet with Her Son,1875, National Gallery of Art, Washington/ Wikimedia Commons/Google Art & Culture; 25: The Studio Boat, 1876, The Barnes Foundation, Philadelphia/ Wikimedia Commons/ ergsap; 27t: The Lunch, 1876-77, Musée d'Orsay, Paris/ Peter Barritt/ Alamy; 31t: The Maneporte (Étretat), 1883, Metropolitan Museum of Art, New York.Bequest of William Church Osborn, 1951/ Wikimedia Commons; 33t: Grainstacks at Giverny, Sunset, 1888-9, Museum of Modern Art, Saitama/ Wikimedia Commons/wikipaintings; 35t: The Main Path Through the Garden at Giverny, c.1901, Osterreichesche Galerie Belvedere, Vienna/ Classic Stock/Alamy; 37: Rouen Cathedral, the Portal, Sunlight, 1894, Metropolitan Museum of Art, New York, Theodora M Davis Collection, Bequest of Theodore M Davis, 1915/ Wikimedia Commons /Postdif; 39: Waterlilies and the Japanese Bridge, 1897-8, Princetown University Art Museum/ Pictorial Press/ Alamy; 41t: Waterloo Bridge, Overcast Weather, 1904, Private Collection/ Wikimedia Commons; 43t: The Japanese Footbridge, 1920-22, Minneapolis Institute of Arts, Bequest of Putnam Dana McMillan/ Wikimedia Commons/MIA; 45t and 46-47t. The Water Lilies: Morning with Willows, 1915-26. Musée de L'Orangerie, Paris. Incamerastock/Alamy.

Quotes:

5, 6: Interview with Francois Thiebault-Sisson, 1900, Claude Monet, An Interview: 1900, Kessinger Publishing, 2009; 8: Letter to Eugene Boudin, August 1892, Monet by Himself: Paintings, Drawings, Pastels, Letters, Chartwell Books, 2014; 10: Letter to Gustav Geffroy, May 1920, Monet by Himself: Paintings, Drawings, Pastels, Letters, Chartwell Books, 2014; 12: Letter to Edouard Manet, 28 June 1875, Monet by Himself: Paintings, Drawings, Pastels, Letters, Chartwell Books, 2014; 14: Letter to J Bernheim-Jeune 10 February 1915, Monet by Himself: Paintings, Drawings, Pastels, Letters, Chartwell Books, 2014; 16: Letter to Alice Hoschede, September 1886, Monet by Himself: Paintings, Drawings, Pastels, Letters, Chartwell Books, 2014; 18: Letter Alice Monet, February 1901, Monet by Himself: Paintings, Drawings, Pastels, Letters, Chartwell Books, 2014; 20: Letter to an unnamed journalist, March 1883, Monet by Himself: Paintings, Drawings, Pastels, Letters, Chartwell Books, 2014; 22: Letter to Frederic Bazille, December 1868, Monet by Himself: Paintings, Drawings, Pastels, Letters, Chartwell Books, 2014; 24: Monet by Himself: Paintings, Drawings, Pastels, Letters, Chartwell Books, 2014; 26: Letter to Paul Durand-Ruel 27 July 1883, Monet by Himself: Paintings, Drawings, Pastels, Letters, Chartwell Books, 2014; 28: Interview with Lilla Cabot Perry, The American Magazine of Art, March 1927 p120; 30: Letter to Alice Hoschede, 27 November 1885, Monet by Himself: Paintings, Drawings, Pastels, Letters, Chartwell Books, 2014; 32: Letter to Alice Hoschede, 3 February 1884, Monet by Himself: Paintings, Drawings, Pastels, Letters, Chartwell Books, 2014; 34: Letter to his gardener, February 1900, Monet by Himself: Paintings, Drawings, Pastels, Letters, Chartwell Books, 2014; 36: Letter to Alice Monet, February 1893, Monet by Himself: Paintings, Drawings, Pastels, Letters, Chartwell Books, 2014; 38: Letter to a French Official, 17 July 1893, Monet by Himself: Paintings, Drawings, Pastels, Letters, Chartwell Books, 2014; 40: Letter to Alice Monet, 26 February 1900, Monet by Himself: Paintings, Drawings, Pastels, Letters, Chartwell Books, 2014; 42: Letter to G Bernheim-Jeune, 11 August 1922, Monet by Himself: Paintings, Drawings, Pastels, Letters, Chartwell Books, 2014; 44: Letter to Gustave Geffroy 1908, Monet by Himself: Paintings, Drawings, Pastels, Letters, Chartwell Books, 2014; 46: Letter to Frederic Bazille December 1868, Monet by Himself: Paintings, Drawings, Pastels, Letters, Chartwell Books, 2014.

HB ISBN 978 1 4451 5611 8
PB ISBN 978 1 4451 5610 1
EBK ISBN 978 1 4451 9529 2

Printed in China.

Franklin Watts
An imprint of Hachette Children's Group
Part of the Watts Publishing Group, Carmelite House,
50 Victoria Embankment, London, EC4Y 0DZ

An Hachette UK Company
www.hachette.co.uk

The authorised representative in the EEA is Hachette Ireland, 8 Castlecourt Centre, Dublin 15, D15 XTP3, Ireland (email: info@hbgi.ie)